Even the beggars have pearls

PETER WYTON

TEMPUS

First published 2001

PUBLISHED IN THE UNITED KINGDOM BY:

Tempus Publishing Ltd
The Mill, Brimscombe Port
Stroud, Gloucestershire GL5 2QG

PUBLISHED IN THE UNITED STATES OF AMERICA BY:

Arcadia Publishing Inc.
A division of Tempus Publishing Inc.
2 Cumberland Street
Charleston, SC 29401
1-888-313-2665

Tempus books are available in France, Germany and Belgium
from the following addresses:

Tempus Publishing Group	Tempus Publishing Group	Tempus Publishing Group
21 Avenue de la République	Gustav-Adolf-Straße 3	Place de L'Alma 4/5
37300 Joué-lès-Tours	99084 Erfurt	1200 Brussels
FRANCE	GERMANY	BELGIUM

British Library Cataloguing in Publication Data.
A catalogue record for this book is available from the British Library.

ISBN 0 7524 1921 8

Typesetting and origination by Tempus Publishing.
PRINTED AND BOUND IN GREAT BRITAIN

- 8 JAN 2007		
2 7 1 u 7		

CUMBRIA LIBRARY SERVICES

Cumbria
COUNTY COUNCIL

This book is due to be returned on or before the last date above. It may be renewed by personal application, post or telephone, if not in demand.

C.L.18

Peter Wyton is backed
(and fronted!)
by
Simon Drew Designs
at
Plugprints
9a Foss Street
Dartmouth
TQ6 9DW

Tel: 01803 833535

Email: plugprints@simondrew.co.uk

Contents

3. Even the beggars have pearls

Previous collections

1993 *Ross Market Poet*, Spectrum RL, Cheltenham

1997 *The Future Dances*, The National Poetry Foundation, Fareham

1999 *Last of the Late Developers*, Trimingham Press, Cheltenham

Some of the poems in *Even the Beggars Have Pearls* have previously appeared in the following publications:

A Book of Ours, *The Express* Newspaper, 1997 Forward Anthology, Headlock, Iota, Lancaster Literature Festival Anthology, Outposts, Purple Patch, Ripley Anthology, Seam, Smiths Knoll, Staple.

Peter Wyton expresses his appreciation for the encouragement and assistance rendered to him by the staff of Tempus Publishing, in particular Steve Lambe and Anne Phipps.

Jacket design and interior artwork by Della Cantillion

Foreword

How many of us write poetry? Many of my friends have 'come out' after the second bottle of chilled white. We tended to write angst-filled odes, in our teenage years. The muse wanes as the mortgage takes hold and only in times of deep sorrow or great happiness do we pick up our pens again. But then there are people like Peter Wyton who had his first piece read on children's radio and never stopped. For the last couple of years I have given up eating chocolate and a poetry collection has replaced my milk chocolate selection. It's hard to save the 'hazelnut whirl' until last when there is no illustrated guide. The best bit is that I must try them all to find the favourite, and then there is the pure joy of tasting them all again.

Peter Wyton has a very broad canvas — those of you who only know him from his many performance poems will be delighted to find this other facet of his work. I met him when we were both taking part in the first Ledbury Poetry Festival in 1997; a couple of years later we shared the stage at the Swindon Literature Festival, when we competed in the Poetry Slam. He beat me by one point — not that I'm bitter.

Even the most casual reader will soon grasp his strong military influences. At first glance, a CV which features 36 years in the RAF would not necessarily predispose one to become a wordsmith. The old axiom 'write about something you know' is well utilised by Peter, but instead of vainglorious odes to war, he gives us a sensitive view. He takes a wry nod at the pomp and circumstance and the military underbelly is revealed, a 'bed-pack a hand-sculpted liquorice allsort' will be with me every time I eat my favourite sweets.

Away from the military, two poems, although very different, touched me deeply. Showing his versatility, 'Keeping In Touch' is a contemporary piece, which will give many readers pause for thought. 'Indescribable' left me stunned as I looked at the over-stuffed sewing box which belonged to my Mother. It is a classic example of how a poem can be so instantly personal. His subject matter is diverse; he dips into history, and makes us look again at childhood and family life. The natural world and its sometimes uncomfortable juxtaposition with humankind, is also taken apart and re-woven in his style.

Peter says that poetry is a constant itch which he needs to keep scratching. Long may it be so.

Wincey Willis

1. committed to the ground

Committed to the ground

Hepialus humuli, commonly, the ghost swift,
hovers in pendulum mode, attracting a mate,
sole light-source in the darkening graveyard.

Immature *Homo Sapiens,* Darren and Tracey,
on the knotted bench in the lych-gate,
lip-riveted, still as a Rodin sculpture.

The moths lately liberated
from two years caterpillar delinquency,
to the detriment of verger's gladioli.

The adolescents on an early learning curve,
eager to shed chrysalis of innocence,
impeded by sheer lack of experience.

Two creatures achieving their life-purpose,
the gossamer union consummated in seconds,
airborne, inches above a weathered tombstone.

A fumbling rite of passage between youngsters
with years of practice ahead of them,
but scant guarantee of fulfillment.

And the sacred earth around them, home
to the husks and the dust of humans and insects,
passively awaiting these disparate couples,
sooner or later, *world without end. Amen.*

Indescribable

Nothing we do can ever bring them back,
those who seemed hugely old when we were young.
Ladies in unrelieved, funereal black,
may glare from photographs, but not give tongue

to the outmoded phrases which they used,
"I have had an ample sufficiency,"
my grandmother intoned, as she refused
another cake, a second cup of tea.

Though we hoard sewing boxes which they prized,
display their carriage clocks upon our shelves,
no preservationist has yet devised
a way of pickling their long-lost Selves.

Unfeatured on the cinematograph,
entombed decades before the video,
memory alone could not imprison half

the attitudes we'd dearly love to show
our kids, although they'd only laugh
and say, "How fossilised." At least they'd *know!*

Birth-flight of a butterfly

Mozart out of the womb, composing;
Napoleon plotting battles at the breast;
Shakespeare in swaddling clothes,
fingers fumbling for the quill;
not one of them quicker off the mark
than this fast-track graduate from the cocoon,
ascending through undisturbed air,
on urgent wings, in a silent warehouse,
erratic flight-path a scrawled signature
on a CV for a job stipulating *NO TIME-WASTERS*.
At the initial obstacle of double-glazing,
rage, as opposed to panic, ensues.
Breeze-blocks, tensile ceiling strength
are tested in pocket-Herculean effort.
Loading bay door yawns, admitting
cacophany of arc-welding, fringed with birdsong.
The butterfly erupts into sunshine,
a flimsy bat out of hell, air-dancing over concrete,
faithful to the creed of Harley-Davidson:
Full throttle to oblivion, nothing less will do.

St Mary's Mill at Chalford

Still stands the mill, monolith from an
industrial past, straddling the valley bed.
Enduring Cotswold stone memorialises
previous employees, the innominate dead.

Broadcloth was woven here, Gloucestershire's
early wealth, a source of local pride.
Stroud-water scarlet stiffened redcoat backs
in every outpost Queen Victoria's soldiers occupied.

Later the product changed. Walking sticks
to enhance the upright citizen.
The Chalford brolly, part and parcel of that uniform
modelled by bowler-hatted city businessmen.

Today, computers hum within stout walls
where looms reverberated. Fax
machines and photocopiers replace old work benches.
Fresh-printed publications stand in shiny stacks.

In basement gloom, undershot water-wheel
and steam beam engine wait the call to fill
some future energy gap. The servant stream flows
as it has for centuries. Still stands the mill.

Night roost

Your first teeth aggravate. My foot
propels the pram wheel back
and forth. You grizzle.
I read Audubon. It's 2am.

If we were guillemots, my son,
this house, my chair, the bed
on which your mother sleeps
upstairs, would be superfluous.

You would have fought your way out of
a pear-shaped egg on four
square inches of Clo Mor
or Ailsa Craig in slanting rain

and forty knots of wind. I would
have sat on you, my beak
and body your defence
against those black-backed cannibals

hovering ceaselessly, just out
of pecking range, watchful
for unprotected chicks,
whilst Mum went bargain-hunting in

the supermarket sea, coming
home weary and crop full.
One consequential day
we would have waddled, you and I,

to where a lip of granite gave
a dizzy prospect of
your future. You'd have stared
at it, at me, then jumped, a small

unguided missile plummeting
three hundred feet — nursery,
primary and secondary
education passed in moments.

I would have screamed encouragement,
swooped down to where you bobbed
bewildered in the waves.
We'd paddle outwards from the cliffs,

you in your stark new element,
cork buoyant in my wake,
the learning curve of an
arctic wave your finishing school.

Tiredness and teething gel combine
to pacify, at length,
my fledgling boy. Book closed,
lights dimmed, I wing my way to bed.

Snug

Concealed in an Everest of bedclothes,
I hibernated through childhood winters,
a cosy prisoner in a quilted penitentiary,
spindly gristle in a flannelette, multi-deck
sandwich, strata of blankets, eiderdown,
bedspread, topped off with optional cat.

Pyjama-clad Sherpa, I emerged daily, eyelid
by cautious eyelid, in a glacial dawn,
to window panes frieze-panelled in icy embroidery.
Toes, traumatised by initial contact with linoleum,
impelled me to the kitchen fireplace via
a chicane of clothes-horses, ponderous adults.

Socks and vest lay ready-toasted on the fender.
Shirt and pants spread-eagled the fireguard.
Tea-pot and porridge bowl simmered in the grate.
Nowadays it's all duvets, labour-saving,
acquiescent drapes, moulding to you in slumber,
amenable to unconscious movement.

In the future we'll be equally comfortable,
muffled in wafer-thin sheets, invented
originally for the protection of spacemen.
Thereafter interest wanes. I shall require
a coffin-pillow only, grave-clothes, a grass counterpane.
At length, to be part of the earth's own bedding.

The vole behind the runway light

A Nimrod taxies. Birds take flight.
Behind barbed wire a hare streaks.
The weasel on the tarmac seeks
the vole behind the runway light.

Fingers of dawn edge down to draw
night's blanket from the aerodrome.
The squadron cat meanders home.
Pale sunlight flicks the hangar door.

The plane lines up, crescendo din
panics the vole. She doubles back
along the asphalt peri-track.
Weasel, spring-loaded, muscles in.

One hunter thunders on its way,
mustering speed to gain the air.
The other, blessed with natural flair,
launches itself towards its prey.

Beyond the Nissen storage sheds
technology and teeth attain
their swaggering triumphs once again.
A jet in flight. A life in shreds.

Old boroughs never die

When Winchcombe was a county
and Stratford was a ford,
each villein, thane and freeman
bent his knee before his lord,
and the accents of the locals
had an Anglo-Saxon lilt,
when Winchcombe was a county
and Bristol wasn't built.

When Winchcombe had an abbey
and Birmingham was fields,
God-fearing men subsisted
on prayer and harvest yields.
Dark forests clothed the countryside
and winter-times were harsh,
when Winchcombe had an abbey
and Moreton had a marsh.

When Winchcombe was a capital
and Gloucester was a fort,
the Hwicce ruled their kingdom,
according to report,
and the fastest thing on wheels was
a one-horse-power chariot,
when Winchcombe was a capital
and Cheltenham was — not!

Almost of Aquitaine

'She was a queen surpassing almost all the queens of the world.'

*Quote from the necrology written in honour of Queen Eleanor, in
the abbey of Notre-Dame de Fontevrault, where she lies buried.*

She wouldn't have liked the 'almost', nuns of Fontevrault,
she who could order a flaying *and* witness its execution.
Well for you she was safely entombed, before you put quill
to parchment! Just out of interest, whom did you value above her?
A virgin, perhaps? Not many of those tripping, crowned, through
the courts of Europe, before or since. We had one in England once,
but come to consider it, *her* credentials were nebulous.
Feisty Eleanor, touchstone for damsels aspiring to girl-power,
romping around on Crusade to the chagrin of wimpish Louis,
marriage annulled by the Pope, then wedded and bedded
with gusto by Henry Plantaganet. Five Princes, three princesses
churned from the royal production loins in a dozen years.
Prudish Fontevrault sisters, think of the congress and shudder!

The females, alliance material, bait for diplomacy.
Boy-children, Eleanor's whelps, coursing the continent,
dragging down kingdoms, snarling at siblings over the bones
of the kill, baring their fangs even at whipper-in Henry.
Cloistered ladies, under your feet lies the dust of a driving force
which fashioned the fabric of life as we know it in newfangled nations,
yet still found time to encourage the arts, her court at Poitiers
brimful of troubadours, music and dancing at all hours.
Thereafter the dungeon years, immured in a motley of moated prisons,
rescued at last by the death of an ill-disposed husband,
the love of a favoured son, to go on intriguing, plotting,
fighting her corner as long as her health permitted.
Here was no fairytale Princess, recluses of Fontevrault.
At the moment of death, you could scarcely imagine her equal.
Eight hundred years on, we cannot better your judgement.
Pray for her soul, but remember, she wouldn't have liked the 'almost'.

Fair Rosamund's choice

Rosamund Clifford's figure and face
took a king's eye and a queen's place
in a royal bed. Beautiful doe,
out of her depth in the ebb and flow
of regal intrigue and imbroglio,
swept away by the undertow.

Dagger or bowl. Dagger or bowl.
Either way, I will never grow old.
Majesty visits, majesty stays
in the bawdy house of his private maze.
I'm the courtesan of a potent man,
but in *this* brothel, the *woman* pays.

Cooped-up lovebird, condemned to dust
by feminine hatred and masculine lust.
From the sally-port of her fortalice,
the Queen of England, the Queen of malice,
bears a honed blade and a poisoned chalice
to her enemy at Woodstock palace.

Dagger or bowl. Dagger or bowl.
Either way, you will never grow old.
My husband's mistress, my life's bane,
pay the price of a wife's pain.
Take your pick. Tipple or prick.
Says Eleanor of Aquitaine.

Metal's kiss or venom's bite.
Which lover takes my body tonight?

Dagger or bowl. Dagger or bowl.
Either way, I will never grow old.

Peasant recipes

Fish of the Irish shoreline; gilpin, grunts,
pollen alive and kicking in the cart,
ling laid out across hedge tops after salting.
Herring grilled over turf, eels to be skinned alive.

Beestings, to be strained from the third milking
into a pie-dish, placed in a cool oven,
left several hours until decently thick,
the curd cut across and across, the whey drained off.

Flummery — otherwise oatmeal blancmange
put through a horse-hair sieve, then to be stirred
with a pot-stick. Take it with what you like.
It eats very pretty with cider and sugar.

Mock goose, joking name for a pig's stomach,
labourers perks after the slaughtering,
scrubbed inside and outside with a hard brush,
loosely filled with potato and onion stuffing.

Carrageen moss, given to calves, or to
dyspeptic humans for the iodine.
Dulce, cut from the rocks at low tide, dried
on the shingle, good for killing the worms in children.

Broth with bacon, poor man's Christmas dinner.
Boxty dumplings, 'specially on Halloween.
Champ for Lenten dinner, hot treacle farls
and buttermilk pancakes griddled for Shrove Tuesday.

Now Titty's gone

Now Titty's gone, stout Able-Seamen grieve
in quay-side bars from Shanghai to the Clyde,
wash down their pemmican with grog and leave,
crew mutinous, bo'suns dissatisfied.

It's years since Arthur went out with the tide.
Old Peter Duck was only make-believe
and even Captain Flint has upped and died.
Now Titty's gone, stout Able-Seamen grieve

and rummage through their memories to retrieve
the pillow-voyages they made beside
their ship-mates. Reminiscences unweave
in quay-side bars from Shanghai to the Clyde.

A knicker-bocker-breaker *is* a slide.
Refute this in your cups and you'll perceive
such Ransomites as have an ounce of pride
wash down their pemmican with grog, and leave.

Jibooms and bobstays! Nancy won't reprieve
bilge rats who mock the yarns we've glorified.
Maroon them on an isolated reef,
crew mutinous, bo'suns dissatisfied.

How many lonely kids identified
with Swallows and Amazons? In dreams, we've
signed aboard from slums and semis nationwide.
Today, collectively, we're *all* bereaved,
now Titty's gone.

Duskfall

The day lies derelict. Low wattage light
of evening permeates flat farming land.
Hoarse rooks retreat before impending night.

Expectant pony takes his patient stand
under the gnarled tree by the paddock gate,
awaiting bucket-clang and beckoning hand.

A vandal mole begins to excavate
that sacred turf, our village bowling green,
blind to the spade-stab of avenging fate.

Proud owner of the last out-door latrine
in England shuffles, hawking, towards his throne,
doffing red braces like a striptease queen.

Darkness prevails. A questing owl alone
attends the unanswered public telephone.

1962

Amnesty International was founded.
The Cuban missile crisis came and went.
Marilyn Monroe took an overdose in Hollywood.
The Sunday Times launched a colour supplement.
James Hanratty and Adolf Eichmann were executed.
The last Gentleman versus Players match took place.
Private Eye was saved from closure by Peter Cook.
The Telstar satellite went into space.
A postman earned ten pounds, two shillings and sixpence
per week. A mechanic, twelve. A shopgirl, maybe, seven.
A posh frock would have set her back nine guineas,
a decent pair of stockings, four-and-eleven.
The local paper in an English country town
ran a modest advert. Some posters were exhibited:
"By kind permission of the Council — for one night only.
Stiletto heels and Teddy boys prohibited."

And The Beatles played in Stroud Subscription Rooms.

Benjamin Britten's *War Requiem* had its premiere.
Khrushchev complained that he didn't understand jazz.
Gary Powers was freed from a Soviet prison.
Three convicts swam to freedom from Alcatraz.
TV showed: *The Origins of Man*, *Z-cars*,
Steptoe & Son, space probes in transit to the moon,
Dr Finlay and *That Was The Week That Was*.
On radio, *Mrs Dale's Diary* got a new signature tune.
A brand new bungalow might be had for a couple of thousand,
a terraced house, half that. The thrifty
and the Do It Yourself enthusiasts could still
find a remote village cottage for a hundred-and-fifty.
Typhoo Tea cost one-and-sixpence a packet.
Heinz baked beans were sevenpence a can.
Tuppence bought a child its weekly ration
of Korky, Dennis the Menace and Desperate Dan.

And The Beatles played in Stroud Subscription Rooms.

Harold Macmillan sacked seven cabinet ministers.
Oistrakh and Menuhin played the Royal Albert Hall.
Chris Bonington climbed the north face of the Eiger.
There were violent mass protests at the Berlin Wall.
The Liberals won the Orpington by-election.
The first De Havilland Trident took to the air.
Yves St Laurent opened his couture house in Paris.
CND members sat down in Parliament Square.
Joan, Jean and Pam came in by bus from Dursley.
Dave, Phil and Mike marched down from Butterrow.
Geoff offered Susie a lift on his Vespa scooter
and sulked when she said she'd walk with her best friend Flo.
There were girls from Rodborough and Paganhill
and lads from Slad and Minchinhampton
crowding the pavements in a jostling, boisterous queue
with teenagers from as far afield as Cam and Frampton.

And The Beatles played in Stroud Subscription Rooms.

Bum-warmers, winkle-pickers and beehive hairstyles.
The Twist, the Mashed Potato and the Locomotion.
Four slim musicians on the treadmill to stardom.
An old building in a state of rare commotion.
The only stimulant in the place was alcohol.
The only drug on the dance floor was nicotine.
Later that evening, word has it that Paul McCartney
walked a local beauty home to Cashes Green

When The Beatles played in Stroud Subscription Rooms.

2. Defensive manoeuvres

Defensive manoeuvres

The prats don't matter. She can handle them.
Quick-feel merchants, bottom-gropers at
the NAAFI servery when her hands are full.
Not just a pretty face, she paid attention
during unarmed combat lessons, knows how
to brace deceptively slim fingers,
jab just where it hurts. Even a slimy senior NCO,
cocking cold weapons of authority,
(Let's not forget who's writing your Report now, darling)
fails to faze her. What she really hates is
the moon madness which occasionally afflicts
lads she has known and liked since Basic Training.
How can they switch from buddy-buddy mode
to lust-filled loon with effortless rapidity?
Always the ambush comes as a complete surprise
to her, on Battle Camp, or in some dark, off-duty night spot.
Breach of trust stabs her like steel. Then, ironically,
she blames herself, ("Did I say something that
he took to mean . . ?"). Beleagured soldier,
trained to defend herself against the foe,
fearful of flak from so-called friendly fire.

Rogue River

Plinlymon spawns me, Sharpness chucks me out,
yet in between times, boy, the fun I've had!
No one can cope with a meander-lout!

I drive their clever flood-control freaks mad.
The half-wits think they have me banked to rights,
but good intentions can't stop *me* being bad.

The hooligan who gives them sleepless nights,
I burst my banks, barge in and burgle theirs,
dance upon doorsteps, choreograph the sights

which swamp their T.V. channels; engulfed squares
and avenues; dank, inundated shops;
relentless waterfalls on cellar stairs.

They ring the rescue teams. They call the cops
while I get — well — not *very* clean away,
leaving them to their sandbags and their mops.

At Bewdley, Stourport, Worcester, Tewkesbury,
disdaining all restraining orders, I
release myself into the community.

A bigger ruffian than Thames or Wye,
I mug 'em all — priest, poet, printer,
Samaritan or callous passer-by.

A lamb in summertime. A lion in winter.
The bad company folk keep falling into.
Cherish me or curse me, I am Severn.
The river that will never get to heaven.

Taking the shine off

Dusting the medals down. First, Long Service
& Good Conduct, traditionally referred to
as 'The undiscovered crime award.'
Next, war gongs. British, unassuming,
sandy ribboned. Saudi, ostentatious
in its cushioned case. Kuwaiti, 4th class tat.
A prial memorialising several weeks
of concentrated conflict, exhausting
in its fashion yet, at least in my case,
scarcely fraught with serious discomfort.

Father-in-law's more worthwhile decorations
mock gently from his widow's tidy dresser.
He marched from Cairo to North Italy
for one more bauble than this clutch I polish,
came home and kept his trap shut,
buried bad memories as he planted fruit trees,
with neither fuss nor flourish.
Not a reunion man. Caroused with no old comrades.
Never slow-marched across the Albert Hall
beneath the Legion Standards and the poppies.

His medals outshine mine. His six year stint
eclipses my three decades under arms.
A better man than me or, come to think of it,
my sire who, having triggered my existence,
heard the responding fusillade of consequence,
ducked from the firing line, deserted.

Regular as clockwork

On Tuesdays, and only on Tuesdays, mind,
make sure you come off shift prompt at 2 a.m.
by the World Service pips. Cross the car park,
go through the gap in the perimeter fencing,
the one the baboons made. Keep straight ahead.
You'll have the fighter dispersal on your left,
the half-built hangars on your right
until you go over the edge of the scarp.
In fifty paces you'll cut loose from the whole shebang,
generator hum, security lights, construction racket.
By the time you reach the clapped out pick-up,
you'll have your night vision. In your one o'clock,
there'll be a big rock, loaf-shaped. Climb it
from the right hand side. There's a thorn thing
on the left that'll rip you to shreds, if you fall in it.
On top look for a hollow place where the lizards sit,
big bastards with greeny-blue faces and paws,
but they'll be long gone by the time you get there.
If you've not dawdled, you should have no more
than five minutes to wait. The lead animal always
has a bloke on top, and another walking at the head.
The last's a bit like a guard's van, guy sitting on a box.
In between, it's just camel after camel after camel,
with a loopy rope dangling between them,
and salt sacks hanging down, each side of the hump,
like udders. I've tried counting, scores of times,
but you lose track somehow. It's the way they sway.
I've timed them though. It takes anything from
fifteen to twenty minutes for a caravan to track by.
Now and then there's a boy running, but not always.
The odd time I've seen a woman, riding.
Woman. Girl. Hard to tell, really, sat bolt upright
like a Guinness bottle. Never a word from any of them,
just the occasional grunt or spit from one of the beasts,
and the moon hanging up there like a gong,
and the stars like you've never seen stars,
and the bondu dogs yapping in the distance.
It's as if you've opened the Old Testament, and crept inside.

A question of attitude

The Namibian fog basket beetle
stands on its head in the desert at dawn,
waving its legs in the air,
so the dew of an African morning
trickles delectably
down from its hips to its lips.

The diminutive stallholder
rocks on his heels in the market at Ross-on-Wye,
slappng his ribs with his arms,
whilst chilly south Herefordshire
creeps irresistibly up
from his soles to his soul.

It's distastefully hard to admit
that an upside-down, bug-eyed grub
may so order its existence
to its complete satisfaction, whilst I,
ostensibly upright,
teeter through the strife of life.

Slow-marching in Lincoln Cathedral

Despite intense organ bombardment, trumpet blast,
shrapnel of massed choirs screaming overhead,
we advance with caution along an aisle pitted,
pockmarked like a scaled-down wartime runway,
under the unified glare of a thousand veteran eyes,
in ambush behind bifocals and Orders of Service,
willing us to shoot ourselves in the Drill Manual foot,
to harpoon the Dean on the Staff of our Squadron Standard,
or commit some comparable breach of military etiquette
which they can tut-tut over afterwards, in the pub.

Defending the altar, a platoon of padres
with fixed hymnals are flanked by the big guns
of the Lord Lieutenant, the Mayor, M.P.s,
reinforced by cannon fodder of lesser dignitaries,
plus a battalion of brass hats fortifying the chancel.
A battery of television cameras takes aim,
tracking us until we stamp to a halt,
loose off battle honours, retire to safe area, offer up
genuine prayers of thanksgiving for safe deliverance,
surreptitiously watch the next squad going over the top.

Smoking the hose

They found him in a borrowed M.T. vehicle
behind the rifle range, the hose-pipe sagging on his lap,
Notification Of Discharge papers on passenger seat.
Someone switched off the ignition. A runner bolted
to the nearest telephone. Birdsong. Indistinct tramp
of Flights en route to Saturday parade. Ambulance wail...
Once they had stashed him in the morgue,
they went through the procedures. Station Commander,
Air Ministry informed, records inspected. C. of E.
No Next-of-kin. Pre-war enlistment. Mespot. Gibraltar.
Tangmere during Battle of Britain. Post-war, Lebanon.
The Canal Zone. Usual Decorations. Then they opened up
his bunk. Found his possessions properly laid out.
Bed-pack immaculate. Boots bulled. Brass-ware polished.
They wrote an inventory. Socks, service pattern,
pairs, three. Shirts, collarless. Braces, elastic.
Vests, cotton. Drawers, cellular, airmen for the use of.
Buttonstick. Knife, fork, spoon, etc. etc. No mufti.
Everything fitted snugly in the regulation kit-bag,
which they carried down to Stores. A civvy signed for it,
hefted it off the counter, took it round the back
and dumped it in the bay marked Dead Men's Kit.

Made by Grays of Belfast

Plain long-case clock,
standing to attention,
polished and dignified
like a good butler,
serving and observing
successive generations.

Denizen of hallways
in more substantial dwellings.
Centrepiece of one cramped,
outer city tower-block flatlet,
currently quite at home in
semi-detached suburbia.

Birth-date uncertain,
(first saw a specialist in 1839)
has viewed dispassionately
every style of dress
from crinolines to mini-skirts,
from tails to vivid T-shirts.

Perennially on duty,
endowing the whole household
with its steady heartbeat,
issuing sharp reminders,
regulating lifestyles
of all within its call.

Not without faults.
It's strike was deemed
a trifle over-shrill.
We cured that with Elastoplast.
It drags its moments now and then.
We make allowances. Adjustments.

The face has seen more faces
than we ever will, links us
with families long since departed.
Measuring time, it also
surely has *our* measure.
Knows where we've come from. Where we're going.

The tsunami dines out

A secret smile, spreading beneath
the smooth complexion of the sea
at several hundred miles an hour,
expanding inshore out of the blue,
changing expression as it hits the beach,
a greedy maw of infinite appetite,
drooling over holiday hotels,
smacking its lips at citrus groves,
sampling the port, making a meal
of quayside bars and chandleries,
helping itself to infrastructure
and inhabitants impartially,
carving whole cities to the bone,
getting its teeth into private property
and public amenities, capable of
stomaching absolutely anything
from kindergartens to hospices
to cemeteries, not turning its nose up
at slums, rubbish tips, sewage plants.
Eventually, a bloated trencherman,
it staggers back to the ocean bed,
leaving in its unsavoury wake
a surge of carrion, a trickle of looters,
the ripple of approaching rescue services.

Conduct prejudicial

Regional Detention Centre. Newspeak for 'guardroom'.
Surfaces dazed with polish. Brass rubbed raw.
Items of kit laid out on lumpy mattresses.
Each man in denims, at ease, by his cell door.

"Orderly Officer present. Detainees, 'ten-*shun*.
Eyes *front*. Stand *still* . . . I said *still,* Pickering!
Mind out for the one at the very end, sir.
Solvent abuse. Right nutter. Keeps hiccuping."

An infant-under-arms, far too many years ago,
I stood to attention like these fellows,
bed-pack a hand-sculpted liquorice allsort
of blanket, sheet, blanket, sheet, blanket, pillows.

What are these felons in for? Barring the glue sniffer,
traditional crimes. Supping one bevvy
too many, then making mayhem in grot-bars.
Assault. Vandalism. Trashing the NAAFI.

" Any complaints?" . . . silence. A sparrow lands, curious,
between window bars, pauses to take stock
of this tableau. Finds nothing edible.
Flits off. Corporal flits on, with Occurrence Book.

"Dismiss them." Chat with the corporal. Sign to certify
they are neither dead, nor absent, nor ill.
Return to the Mess in time for the phone call . . .
"Sir. Remember the one with the hiccups? Well . . ."

Unmentioned in dispatches

Some of them never come home to fanfares,
they dump their kit-bags down at the door,
kiss their wives and let their children
wrestle them down to the kitchen floor,
switch the telly on, pour out a whiskey,
search for the local football score.

Some of them skip the quayside welcome,
dodge the bunting and cannonade,
make their landfall in silent harbours,
nod to the coastguard, but evade
the searchlight of public scrutiny
like those engaged in the smuggling trade.

Some of them land at lonely airfields
far removed from the celebration,
hang their flying gear in a locker,
cadge a lift to the railway station,
make for home and take for granted
the short-lived thanks of a grateful nation.

Some of them miss the royal salute,
the victory parade along the Mall,
the fly-past, the ships in formation passing
the cheering crowds on the harbour wall.
Remembered only by friends and relatives,
some of them never come home at all.

The cull of the wild

The bulk of the harvest is reaped at night.
Pathetic remains in dismembered piles
discolour the highway by morning light.

The early rising traveller with miles
to cover on country lanes is a shocked
accident witness, a mourner in aisles

consecrated to violent death, pocked
with distorted carcasses of the deer
departed, the badger and fox knocked

off, advantage of sharper eye and ear
over ponderous humankind outweighed
by insidious, paralysing fear

spawned in discordant serenade
of clamorous lorry and motor car,
a gut-wrenching, bone-snapping hit parade

which crushes small creatures onto the tar
and reduces the road to an abattoir.

The unkindest defence cut of all

I'm the last man left in the Air Force,
I've an office in MOD
and a copy of Queens Regulations
which only apply to me.
I can post myself to Leuchars
and detach me from there to Kinloss,
or send me on courses to Innsworth,
then cancel the lot — I'm the boss.

I'm the last man left in the Air Force,
but the great Parliamentary brains
neglected, when cancelling people,
to sell off the Stations and planes.
The result is, my inventory bulges
with KD and camp-stools and Quarters,
plus a signed book of speeches by Trenchard
which I keep to impress the reporters.

I'm the last man left in the Air Force,
I suppose you imagine it's great
to be master of all you survey, but
I tell you it's difficult, mate.
I inspected three units last Thursday,
As AOC (Acting) of Strike,
then I swept half the runway at Laarbruch
and repaired Saxa Vord's station bike.

I'm the last man left in the Air Force,
it's not doing a lot for my health.
Unit sports days are frankly exhausting
when the Victor Ludorum's oneself.
On guest nights the Mess is so lonely,
there are times when I wish I was able
to pass the port to the chap next to me,
without seeing it fall off the table.

I'm the last man left in the Air Force,
my wife says I'm never at home,
when I'm not flying Hercs, I'm at Manston,
laying gallons and gallons of foam,
or I'm in my Marine Craft off Plymouth,
shooting flares at the crowds on the Ho,
or I'm Orderly Corporal at Luqa.
It's an interesting life, but all go.

I'm the last man left in the Air Force.
I'm ADC to the Queen,
I'm Duty Clerk at St. Mawgan,
I'm the RAF rugby team.
Tomorrow I'm painting a guardroom
and air-testing numerous planes.
The day after that I'm for London,
to preach at St. Clement Danes.

I'm the last man left in the Air Force
and I'm due to go out before long.
There's been no talk of any replacement
and I won't even let *me* sign on.
I hope to enjoy my retirement.
I've put up a fairly good show,
and I won't cut myself off entirely.
There are always reunions, you know.

At the end of the killing line

Age: 15. Height 4'9". Status: executive. Evidence:
tie, shoes, clip-board, nervous tic. Duties: weighing,
(in transit, left to right) wheeled vats of kidneys,
hearts, heads, trotters, sweetbreads, (in transit
right to left) clean trolleys, stacked with
shop-bound products. I subtract tare of vehicle
from weight of quivering offal, push periodic slips
through pigeon hole to super-exec in portaphonebox
with own stool. View: tiles, hooks, swinging carcasses,
flashing knives. Leisure activities: lunch break soccer
in loading yard with vat and trolley shovers, all twice
my size, clog-shod, with socialist principles, or else
watching older hands play billiards, in a Capstan Full
Strength cloud, amidst a grunting, coughing scrum.
Places I seldom go, if I can help it: 1. Upstairs,
where there are people in suits. 2. The opposite end
of the killing line, where pigs are individually
stampeded through a channel, underneath a rusted stile,
where the man stands with the fag hanging from his lip,
one eye closed, the long mallet arcing over and down.

Elected local representatives, proposals for the preservation of, committee stage. (Focus group discussion paper)

Be kindly to your Councillor,
he isn't very bright,
or he wouldn't take a job
where you could ring him up at night
to tell him that your drains are blocked
or that your garden gnomes
have been pilfered by a fine arts thief
disguised as Sherlock Holmes.

Be charming to your Chairperson,
don't make your language graphic.
She doesn't dig the roads up
to obstruct commuter traffic.
She doesn't sanction power cuts,
or sever sewerage pipes,
or permit your neighbour's children
to behave like guttersnipes.

Don't vilify your Mayor
when he attends official functions.
His digestion's being ruined
by all those civic luncheons.
Don't make hurtful, cutting comments
when he's robed up to the teeth.
For all you know he might be
drop-dead gorgeous underneath.

Pamper local politicians.
Remember, we elect them,
and it's in our vital interests
to cosset and protect them.
If they feel so undervalued
that they won't get out of bed,
the government might make *us*
all be Councillors instead!

3. Even the beggars have pearls

Even the beggars have pearls

The title (and only the title) is a quote from a Gurkha soldier's letter
home to his family, after arriving in England on his first tour of duty.

Mother, there are no mountains.
Buildings have crushed the horizon.
Vehicles skitter like lizards through
slits between concrete and steel.

In the cities, cameras on stalks
monitor movement, so nobody
needs to pay any attention
to burglar alarms and nobody does.

Our English instructor says paté
routinely is spread on the crusts
of the poor, but he cannot afford it.
The ghettos have satellite dishes.

Temples lie empty. The priests play
on one-arm bandits, or spit in the parks.
They pray into mobile phones.
Their faces are pitted with metal.

All the children have wheels on their feet.
They scribble their homework
on bridges and walls, so the teachers
may mark it while travelling to school.

Today is Lectures. Tomorrow
is Salisbury Plain. I have bought you
a pop-up book of the Queen's Dolls House
at great expense, and my sister a yo-yo.

Blencarn levies

Many of rural Lancashire's dry stone walls were built by soldiers
recently returned from the Napoleonic wars.

Recruited by upland men in an uphill struggle,
patrolling borders, policing drovers roads.
Shelter for shivering beasts in numbing wind-chill.
Sentries at gateways. Guardians of summer grazing.

Here, where our captains ordered us to attention,
we have done our duty this hundred-and-fifty years.
From the very beginning, our most inveterate enemy
yearly campaigns against us in his season.

Strangers to nails, cement, the welder's blowtorch,
under assault the virtues we value are
comradeship, strength in depth, a sense of belonging.
Either we hang together, or crumble in ruin.

We are local lads, with only a few exceptions.
Specially selected, pasture clearance enlistments,
Disciplined. Drilled by battle-hardened veterans.
Correctly positioned. Smartly dressed in formation.

Some of the older troops have seen previous service.
A few of the footers came from a Roman road.
Our heavy-weight champion, over there by the hogg-hole,
assisted a Norman king to mount his destrier.

Enough of soldiers yarns! Our cam-stone lookouts
warn us of autumn's retreat. Bracing once more,
shoulder to shoulder across the sheep-flecked fellside,
we await the first white salvos of winter war.

Ephemeral

Fullbeam of lovelight starts
roses and hearts
flowering.

Flashfire of passion finds
petals and minds
charring.

Flamejoy to embergrieve
sorrow and sunset leave
the heart smarting
the rose closing.

Bodnant

The gardens at Bodnant in North Wales, run by the National Trust,
are open to the public.

In an Eden of plunging terraces, muscled stonework
shoulders its vibrant burden of climbing roses.
Marching sequoias, towering redwood guardsmen,
trample stiffly over a lush parade-ground.

Pathways implore us to follow them, corners beckon,
coaxing us on through triumphant laburnum arches.
We are lured to beauty spots, tempted towards open prospects
where placid pools lie, jewelled with lily brooches.

Grandeur brings out the best in us. Glacial, the eye
which rests on *magnolia robusta* and does not soften.
If we cannot catch our breath at rhododendrons
massing before us, what is the purpose of breathing?

Buildings occur, suitable to their surroundings.
Nothing intrudes, offends, is out of kilter.
So easy to be a bard in a God-given garden,
where even a mausoleum is known as *The Poem.*

Walking out with Jack Hobbs

Captured in snapshot after snapshot,
marching purposefully to the wicket
down weathered steps, amidst polite applause,
between the serried rows of members chairs,
past schoolboys, desperate for autographs,
they pace together across new-mown grass,
against the backdrops of well-known pavilions
in a variety of nationwide locations:
Headingley. Taunton. Scarborough Festival.
Lords. Trent Bridge. Edgebaston. The Oval.
Disparate couple. One, with guardsman's stride,
familiar to everybody in the crowd,
pre-eminent opening batsman of his time,
six decades later, still a household name.
Perversely then, I focus my attention
on his less illustrious companion,
whose eyes avoid the lens, whose stride is shorter,
in general a step behind The Master.
Neat and methodical. Preoccupied of face,
an artisan in tandem with a genius,
or so it seems until I make a check
upon this fellow-traveller in the record book.
Andy Sandham. Scored more centuries than C.B. Fry,
more runs than Hutton. Curious the way
some stars lose lustre, different ones endure.
He played one thousand first class innings for
his club and country. No more. No less.
Career statistics rounded and precise
as his technique. Oh, to turn back the clock
and see him take the field with mighty Jack.

Stilt-walker at the Edinburgh Festival

Extravagant of gesture, walking tall
on tapered limbs along the esplanade,
acknowledging the watchers on the wall,
outstanding in the colourful parade,

she forms the focus of the cavalcade,
garmented in a silver waterfall
of skin-tight silk. Haughty, grease-painted jade,
extravagant of gesture, walking tall.

Seen afterwards, minus the fol-de-rol
of costume, she seems curiously staid,
scarcely the sort of trollop who might loll
on tapered limbs along the esplanade.

Brought down to earth, her heady masquerade
abandoned, it's perplexing to recall
the Titan she had previously played,
acknowledging the watchers on the wall.

We, the spectators at the carnival,
dream we might emulate the way she swayed,
never the least suggestion of a fall,
outstanding in the colourful parade.

What president, what king would not swap all
his consequence, his wealth, the very braid
upon his hat, to cross his capital
on foot in safety, smiling, unafraid,
extravagant of gesture.

The postillion strikes back

In this 'found poem' the individual sentences have been culled from a diversity of old foreign language books, either featured in translation exercises, or used to illustrate grammatical points.

The masons did not want red umbrellas.
The bandits took themselves off, perplexed
at all the noise. There was fish, but there's none left.
Without collar or scarf, he entered the compound
of the High Court. But we have formed a snowball
of goodly dimensions. I compared my watch
with the noonday gun. Has your coolie brought
sufficient pegs? Do you ever go out for a sham-fight?
I have picked up your razor in the courtyard,
it has not been spoilt much. Hard luck,
they have changed my galoshes. It is evident that
they have beaten an interpreter. If I lampoon him,
he cries out like a nine-year-old camel. This pole
is firmer than that one which we threw away
yesterday. The barber's white donkey kicked my aunt.
You, who will not see the spear, will pass the hut.
I am tired of telling you to water the maidenhead ferns
in the evening. And one's quietus take with a spare bodkin.

Jack Mapanje is gobsmacked

Ledbury Poetry Festival, 1999

His audience is homeward bound, well entertained.
He's done his bit. He's back in Hospitality.
A glass of this, a slice of that, and Jack's in clover,
conversational, transparently impressed.
They've closed the streets for poetry!, he says,
and he is not far wrong. The Festival's *en fete,*
traffic diverted, barricades in place. A salsa band
has just erupted, Trojan style, from a pantechnicon.
Mood music storms the town. The pubs are full,
hip-swinging crowds congest the thoroughfare.
Big mommas sway. Cool dudes gyrate.
Babies with bulging eyes are held aloft
to view the spectacle. Gangs of small boys
rush to and fro, demented ferrets wriggling
through the adult mass. Sometime next week,
next month, maybe next year, on tour in Africa,
or at some arty-farty South Bank bash,
the mention of a small West Midlands town
will jog Jack's memory. He'll slap his thighs.
His chest will heave. He'll roar, *Ah, Ledbury.*
That's where they close the streets for poetry!

Doctor of Signatures

The Doctrine of Signatures, first refered to by Pliny and developed, over centuries, by many pioneers of medicine, held that all healing herbs possess some God-given shape, symbol or colour to indicate their use.

They have muffled the door-knocker, covered
the cobblestones with rushes to smother cart-clatter.
I am to rest in peace, presumably!

The shrillness of house-servants seeing off
street-criers remains audible, as does the twittering
of relatives, adjusting my pillows.

So inert have I become, that I must summon up
a groan from time to time, for fear that my kinsfolk
will inter me prematurely.

Within the collapsed castle of my body,
my mind yet functions; a herbalist, turning over
the leaves of his life in his final hours.

*Wild Thyme: The whole plant is fragrant and yields
an essential oil that is very healing. An infusion
of the leaves removes the head-ache,
occasioned by the debauch of the previous night.*

Soon I shall meet my father. How do I greet
a clergyman in heaven, who died nineteen days
before his gentle wife gave birth to me?

And I may spot my naughty ancestors,
Henry Tudor's fifth queen and her indiscreet cousin,
who paid with their heads for the sins of their loins....

...unless, of course, they are quartered elsewhere,
as I myself may be, come to think of it.
My own life has not been devoid of incident.

I attempted an elopement, fought a duel,
took Parliament's side against the King,
though I regard that as a virtue, not a vice.

Anemone: Called also wind-flower, because they say
the flowers never open but when the wind bloweth;
Pliny is my author; if it be not so, blame him.

When I climb the stairs to St. Peter's gate, I can
but hope that my life's work will weigh in the balance
against the transgressions of my youth.

I have been researcher, apothecary,
astrologer; also turned linguist to translate
the teachings of Galen and Hippocrates.

There is my *Herbal,* my *Health for the Rich*
and Poor, by Diet, without Physick, my treatises
on blood-letting, cupping and scarifying.

Finally I commend my last legacy,
my *Aurum Potabile,* liquid gold, to the judgement
of my Maker and fellow-men.

All-heal: Its root is long, thick and exceeding full
of juice. It provokes the terms, expels the dead-birth.
It is excellent for the griefs of the sinews
and purgeth choler very gently.

This being, I surmise, the last mental utterance of me,
Nicholas Culpeper, in his home at Spittle-fields,
on the East Side, next door to the Red Lyon.

Plumbing is Icumen back,
Lhude sing Armitage-Shanks

I sing the Victorian bathroom. Give me earthenware.
Give me cast iron. Away with your mineral resin compounds,
your sculpted seat-covers, your concealed cisterns.
I want Twyford's 'Deluge', including Basin & Trap,
Slop Top & Paper Box, Galvanised Seat Brackets,
Rubber Connections, plus Pendant Pull, Ivory Handle
& Ebonised Block, only 7/6d extra! Alternatively,
should this be too opulent for my station in life,
give me the patent 'Tornado', strong, cheap and reliable,
in fire clay, with deal seat, suitable for artisans dwellings.
I scorn your swivel spouts, your lotion dispensers,
your power showers with body jet, invigorating massage,
or soft bubbly spray options. Let me wallow
in the steamless and noiseless 'Cleopatra' tub,
Japanned Sienna inside, finished on the outside
(at no extra expense) in Pea-Green, Sea-Green,
Shell-Pink or Rose Antique, with the choice of either
Secret or Tell-Tale overflow and a large outgo
for quick discharge, affording excellent flush to house drain,
weighing, when ready for shipment, 4 cwt. 20 lbs. gross.

Keeping in touch

When shift duties made conversation impracticable
       — she a paramedic, he a traffic cop —
they communicated via fridge magnet.
   ~ DENTAL CHECKS FRIDAY 9am ~ PAY MILK ~
   ~ GET CAT FOOD ~ ~ FORGOT. YOU GET IT! ~
Messages sometimes veered away from the mundane.
He'd proposition her in mock Shakespearean,
   ~ I'LL TUP THEE THIS NIGHT, DIMINUTIVE STRUMPET ~
She'd respond, in fluent Gangster,
   ~ WAKE ME AND YOU'RE HISTORY, YUH BIG PALOOKA ~
For her birthday he concocted a love-letter
twenty-five wobbly lines long, ending with the lament,
   ~ NOT ENOUGH X's ~ Three nights later, she eased him
from the chassis of his shattered squad car,
rushed him to Casualty, came home and knelt before
the cold white altar, ripped off all previous graffito,
laboured until the sun came up, fashioning the mantra
          ~ DON'T LEAVE ME ~
          ~ DON'T LEAVE ME ~
          ~ DON'T LEAVE ME ~
          ~ DON'T LEAVE ME ~
          ~ DON'T LEAVE ME ~
from top to bottom of the pristine door.
News reached her by mobile, three hours later,
just as she left the joke shop in the precinct,
having bought ten new alphabets, just for the X's.

One to one

The obituary of entertainer Rod Hull revealed a wealth
of surprising information about the life of his less famous father.

If I could have a one to one with you, I'd ask
why you spent the better part of your life
chasing jobs for which you were unqualified,
like setting up as a plumber on the strength
of having purchased a plunger from Woolworth's.
I'd be interested in the nitty-gritty of your stint
as a sweeper-up in a glue factory,
your impact on the bicycle-repair industry,
in particular the time you replaced
the district nurse's missing saddle-nut
with one from the handlebars.
We'd discuss your sudden decision
to emigrate to Australia, having never
previously left the Isle of Sheppey,
and your brief career as a door-to-door
purveyor of burial plots, accompanied
by your wife, equipped with portable organ,
on which she played *Rock Of Ages*
as a sales gimmick. It seems a shame
that I'd never even heard of you,
until I read the Telegraph obituary.
Not yours, of course. Your son's.
The one who fell off his roof, adjusting
his aerial during a televised soccer match.
Amazingly, not even the tabloids claimed
that he'd been wearing a raffia emu
on one arm at the time of the accident.

Still-life in the garden

I wait for salmagundi at the kitchen sink,
alert for that seasonal manifestation,
a kind of suburban Condor moment,
fusion of human and natural circumstances

generally occurring after the daffodil days,
before peonies and Canterbury Bells,
in the time of aquilegia
and burgeoning honeysuckle against brickwork.

Timing is important. The dawn chorus terminated.
Birds dispersed to wherever birds go to
when they've done clearing their throats.
Blue sky. A total lack of wind essential.

Add to the potion an absence of traffic,
comatose neighbours (Sunday morning a Best Bet),
no distant trains or droning aircraft,
my fridge not in rattle mode.

When this complex federation
of conditions comes together, my garden
stands to attention like a military parade
immediately prior to the arrival of the V.I.P.

A hundred thousand leaves, totally motionless,
green carapace above honour-guard
of plant pots, dressed across crazy paving.
Poppy medals gleam in the flower beds.

The frogs at the pond's edge find
themselves incapable of obeying the command
"Eyes front!", but otherwise enter
fully into the spirit of the occasion.

For a brief interlude, I am the possessor
of my own Monet, as perfect in its way
as anything in a National Gallery,
a masterpiece in a kitchen window-frame.

Then a magpie shatters illusion,
bombing heavily to the lawn. Trees sway.
A car engine splutters. The battering ram
of Sunday newsprint smashes through the letter-box.